A Century
of Stories
New Hanover County Public Library
1906-2006

OCEANS AND SEAS

ARCTIC OCEAN

Jen Green

WORLD ALMANAC® LIBRARY

Please visit our web site at: www.worldalmanaclibrary.com
For a free color catalog describing World Almanac® Library's list of
high-quality books and multimedia programs, call 1-800-848-2928 (USA)
or 1-800-387-3178 (Canada). World Almanac® Library's fax: (414) 332-3567.

Library of Congress Cataloging-in-Publication Data

Green, Jen.
    Arctic Ocean / Jen Green.
      p. cm. — (Oceans and seas)
    Includes bibliographical references and index.
    ISBN 0-8368-6270-8 (lib. bdg.)
    ISBN 0-8368-6278-3 (softcover)
    1. Arctic Ocean—Juvenile literature. 1. Title.
  GC401.G74   2006
  551.46'132—dc22   2005054135

First published in 2006 by
World Almanac® Library
A Member of the WRC Media Family of Companies
330 West Olive Street, Suite 100
Milwaukee, WI 53212 USA

Produced by Discovery Books
Editor: Sabrina Crewe
Designer and page production: Sabine Beaupré
Photo researcher: Sabrina Crewe
Maps and diagrams: Stefan Chabluk
Geographical consultant: Keith Lye
World Almanac® Library editorial direction: Valerie Weber
World Almanac® Library editor: Gini Holland
World Almanac® Library art direction: Tammy West
World Almanac® Library graphic design: Charlie Dahl
World Almanac® Library production: Jessica Morris and Robert Kraus

Picture credits: Corbis: pp. 10, 12, 30, 39, 41, 43; FLPA: cover, pp. 11, 12 (bottom),
14, 17, 19, 22 (top), 33, 36; Getty Images: pp. 15 (top), 28, 31, 32, 35 (bottom); NOAA:
pp. 6, 13, 16 (both), 20, 23, 25, 29, 40; NOAA/*National Geographic*: p. 8; NOAA/NGDC: title
page; Photodisc: pp. 21 (4), 24; Mark Rauzon: pp. 26, 37, 38; United States Navy: p. 34.

Printed in the United States of America

1 2 3 4 5 6 7 8 9 10 09 08 07 06

CONTENTS

Front cover: *A bearded seal rests on an ice floe in front of a glacier on the Norwegian island of Spitsbergen in the Arctic Ocean.* Title page: *This computer-generated image of Earth was based on land and ocean measurements made by the U.S. National Geophysical Data Center. This view shows the Arctic Ocean in the center (the light blue and dark blue area) with North America below. The orange landmass is the island of Greenland.*

Words that appear in the glossary are printed in **boldface** the first time they occur in text.

The Arctic Ocean is located in the far north of the world in the area around the North Pole, which is the most northern point on Earth. Much of the Arctic Ocean is covered with a thick layer of ice. In the most northern parts of the ocean, the ice never melts. During the long months of winter, the Sun does not rise at the North Pole. In summer, however, the Sun never sets there.

The Arctic Ocean is named after *arktos*, a Greek word meaning bear. The name refers to the star constellation of the Great Bear, or Big Dipper, which shines in the northern sky.

Boundaries of the Arctic Ocean

The Arctic Ocean is the smallest of the world's oceans, about one and a half

---

Icy Waters

"Because so much of its waters are covered with ice, the Arctic Ocean remains the least understood of the world's seas."

Barry Lopez, Arctic Dreams, *1986*

---

times the size of the United States. Most, but not all, of the ocean is located within the **Arctic Circle**, an imaginary line around Earth's most northern region. The ocean is almost entirely surrounded by land, with northern areas of North America, Europe, Russia, and Greenland (the world's largest island and part of the European nation of Denmark) all forming part of the ocean's boundary. Arctic waters mingle with the Pacific Ocean at the Bering **Strait**, the narrow channel of water between Russia and Alaska. The Arctic merges with the Atlantic in the waters east and west of Greenland. The outer waters of the Arctic are divided into seven, mostly shallow, seas: the Barents, Kara, Laptev, East Siberian, Chukchi, Beaufort, and Greenland Seas. The Arctic Ocean also encompasses Baffin Bay and Hudson Bay as well as other waters.

Arctic Ocean Key Facts

Surface area: 5,426,000 square
    miles (14,056,000 sq km)
Average depth: 3,950 ft
    (1,205 meters)
Coastline: 28,205 miles
    (45,389 km)
Deepest known point: 15,305 feet
    (4,665 m), in the Fram Basin
    north of Svalbard

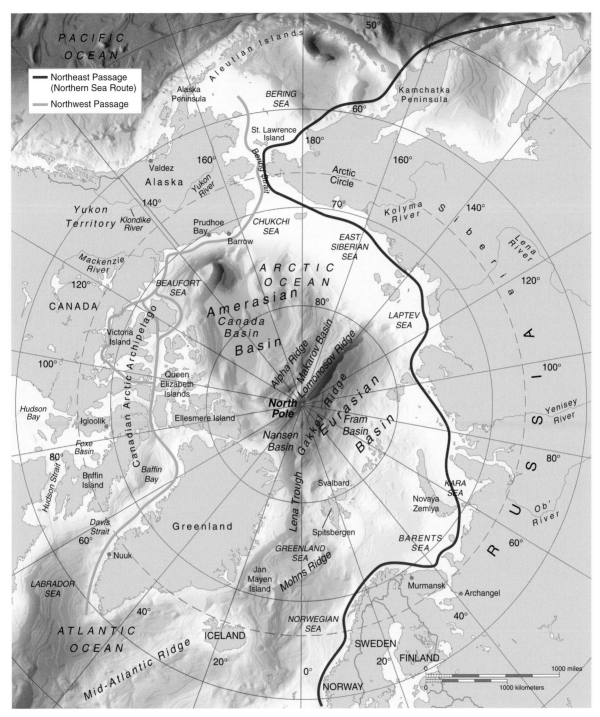

On this map of the Arctic Ocean, north is in the center, not at the top. Everything around the North Pole is south of it.

A Harsh Place

The ice-choked Arctic Ocean is one of the harshest places on Earth, but people have lived on the shores of the ocean for tens of thousands of years. The last three hundred years have brought great changes to the Arctic. People from nations south of the ocean have come to harvest the Arctic's resources, including fish, seals, whales, and—more recently—**minerals**.

CHAPTER ONE

PHYSICAL FEATURES

The Arctic is much shallower than the world's other oceans, with an average depth of 3,950 feet (1,205 m). It has some very deep regions, however. Like all ocean floors, the Arctic bed is far from flat. If all the water drained away, dramatic features, such as high mountain ranges, deep trenches, and volcanoes, would appear. All these features were formed by the slow movement of the giant sections of rock, called tectonic plates, that make up Earth's outer layers. These movements and other factors ensure that the Arctic Ocean is still changing today.

Formation

Scientists believe the Arctic Ocean began to form about one hundred million years ago, as tectonic plates very slowly drifted and jostled in the region. On a plate border that is now the Gakkel **Ridge**, plates drifting in opposite directions created a deep cleft where **magma** welled upward, pushing the rocks on either side apart. Over millions of years, Earth's crust widened here to form the Fram Basin, part of the deep Eurasian Basin between the Gakkel Ridge and what is now the Russian mainland. As tectonic plates continued to move, pressure forced a fragment of the Asian continent to break away and drift north, to form the Lomonosov Ridge. Around the same time, plate movement caused the land-mass of Alaska to swing away from the rest of North America. This opened a new basin, now known as the Canada Basin.

Barrow on the coast of Alaska looks out over the Canada Basin, the largest of the four Arctic Ocean basins. The basin formed because of tectonic plate movement.

Plates and Oceans

Earth's outer layers are made up of a number of vast, rigid sections called tectonic plates—seven major ones and up to twelve smaller ones. Fitting together like pieces of a jigsaw puzzle, the plates underlie oceans and dry land. The plates drift across Earth's surface, floating on a lower, molten layer of the **mantle** like chunks of bread on a thick, bubbling soup. As they drift, tectonic plates can push together, grind past one another, or pull apart.

Volcanic eruptions and earthquakes are common along plate boundaries because the crust is thinnest there. Where two plates pull apart, as they are doing along the Gakkel Ridge in the Arctic, magma rises to fill the space, creating a mountain chain under-water or on land. Elsewhere, plates collide. Where this happens, one plate may dive below the other to form a deep trench, such as the Lena Trough.

About 250 million years ago, Earth's landmasses were united in a single "super-continent" named Pangaea, which was surrounded by a vast ocean now known as Panthalassa. About 200 million years ago, because of **continental drift** caused by plate movement, a great bay—the Tethys Sea—opened up in the center of Pangaea and split it in half. The northern landmass—named Laurasia—included North America, Greenland, Europe, and Asia, while the southern half—Gondwanaland—included South America, Africa, India, Australia, and Antarctica. As plate movement continued over millions of years, the continents and oceans took their present positions (shown below, with the major tectonic plates), and they continue to shift today.

Fossils brought up from the ocean floor show that, about forty million years ago, the Arctic Ocean was considerably warmer than it is today. The ocean has been covered with ice for several million years, but scientists have yet to discover exactly when the ocean cooled.

Mysteries of the Ocean Floor

The geography of the Arctic Ocean floor was completely unknown until the 1940s. Then scientists began to chart the floor with **sonar**—a system using sound waves to measure depth. They also took seabed samples and explored in submarines. The floor of the ocean is still not completely mapped, and submarines cruising the depths still come across new features, including underwater mountains, ridges, and deep trenches. The icy, bitter cold and long months of darkness make exploration difficult. The Arctic Ocean still holds many secrets that have yet to come to light.

Basins and Ridges

Some features of the Arctic floor, however, are well known. The center of the Arctic Ocean is mostly occupied by a deep basin, which is cut by several under-sea ridges running parallel to each other. The highest is the Lomonosov Ridge,

Before sonar, Arctic explorers of the early 1900s used piano wire with a weight at the end for sounding, or measuring ocean depths. These men were taking soundings on Robert Peary's 1908–1909 expedition across the Arctic. Peary returned claiming to have reached the North Pole.

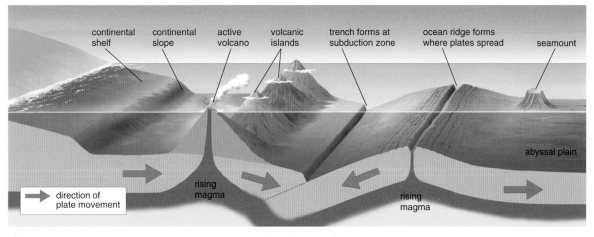

continental shelf

continental slope

active volcano

volcanic islands

trench forms at subduction zone

ocean ridge forms where plates spread

seamount

abyssal plain

rising magma

rising magma

direction of plate movement

This diagram shows some of the features that form on Earth's ocean floors.

discovered by Russian scientists in 1948. This underwater mountain chain rises as much as 10,000 feet (3,000 m) above the seabed. Stretching for 1,100 miles (1,750 km) between Greenland and Siberia, it divides the ocean floor into two main basins: the Amerasian Basin (comprising the Makarov and Canada Basins) and the Eurasian Basin (made up of the Nansen and Fram Basins). Other ridges lie either side of the Lomonosov Ridge: the Alpha Ridge on the North American side and the Gakkel Ridge (also called the Mid-Arctic Ridge) on the Russian side.

Plains and Trenches

The flattish floors of the basins—called abyssal plains—lie mostly about 10,000 to 12,000 feet (3,000 to 3,700 m) below the surface. In places, the bottom drops away to form deep trenches. These are found in areas called **subduction zones**, where two tectonic plates collide and one plate is forced down below the other. The Lena Trough, for example, is a deep

chasm running midway between Greenland and the Norwegian island of Spitsbergen in the Svalbard island group.

Spreading Outward

The Gakkel Ridge is a line of active volcanoes stretching for some 1,100 miles (1,800 km). This undersea mountain chain is the Arctic extension of the Mid-Atlantic Ridge, a very long chain running down the center of the Atlantic Ocean at the boundary between tectonic plates. As plates drift gradually apart along these borders, magma from deep inside Earth wells up to fill the gap, creating ridges cut by deep **rift** valleys. When magma surges up here, it forms new rock that pushes apart the older rock on either side, and the ocean floor gets gradually wider.

In 2001, scientists investigating the Gakkel Ridge discovered that the ocean floor is spreading more slowly there than at other plate margins. It is widening by just 0.4 inches (1 centimeter) each year. Other plate margins in the world are widening by as much as 7.5 inches (19

Hydrothermal Vents

In 1977, scientists exploring the ocean depths in **submersibles** made an amazing discovery. In a rift valley on a deep-ocean ridge in the Pacific, they came upon extraordinary rock chimneys belching clouds of scalding water, black with the minerals sulfur and iron. These hydrothermal vents, also called "black smokers," are now thought to occur in volcanically active regions in many parts of the oceans, including on the Gakkel Ridge and Mohns Ridge in the Arctic Ocean. At these sites, ocean water entering cracks in the crust is heated and mixed with newly erupted minerals to gush out again in dark clouds of hot water. The minerals settle and build up around the vents to form chimneys. They also seep out into the ocean, adding to the water's salt levels. "White smokers" have also been found. These vents spew slightly cooler water containing white minerals.

The long, frozen coastline of Siberia slopes gradually down into the Arctic's continental shelf.

cm) per year.

Volcanic activity along the Gakkel Ridge causes the formation of **hydrothermal vents**. These cracks in the ocean floor spout clouds of black, superheated water.

Continental Shelves

Around the borders of seas and oceans, undersea ledges called continental shelves edge the world's great land-masses. On these gently sloping ledges, the waters are generally less than 500 feet (152 m) deep. The continental shelves of the Arctic are an important feature, being wider than those of any other ocean. In fact, they take up one-third of the whole ocean floor. The shelves off Siberia stretch up to 990 miles (1,600 km) into the ocean. Off Canada and Alaska, they are much narrower, only 60–125 miles (100–200 km) wide. The vast extent of these coastal shallows explains why the Arctic is, on average, the world's shallowest ocean.

Oceanic Islands

Two main kinds of islands are found in oceans worldwide: oceanic islands and continental islands. Oceanic islands, often found far out to sea, are mostly formed by volcanoes erupting on the ocean bed. If the eruption continues for long enough, the **lava** builds up to form an island. The large island of Iceland lies on the Mid-Atlantic Ridge with part of its northern coastline just inside the Arctic Circle. It has many active volcanoes, hot springs, and geysers—natural fountains spouting scalding-hot water.

These features are formed by water seeping into volcanically active areas below ground. Another volcanic island is the Norwegian island of Jan Mayen, situated in the Arctic Ocean north of Iceland. This barren, uninhabited island formed around the extinct volcano Mount Beerenberg, which rises 7,450 feet (2,270 m) above sea level.

Continental Islands

Most islands in the Arctic Ocean are continental islands. These mainly lie close to continents, and indeed they were once part of the mainland when sea levels were lower. Sea levels are lower during long, cold periods called ice ages, when

*Spitsbergen was named by Dutch explorers—the word means "pointed mountains"—and is a continental island in the Svalbard group of islands. It was formed by changes in sea level and shaped by glacial activity. The land in the foreground is known as **tundra**, where the subsoil is always frozen.*

Glaciers, such as the one above on Ellesmere Island, carve the land to form valleys as they move toward the sea. Valleys filled with ocean water become fjords, such as Geiranger Fjord in Norway (right).

much of Earth's water is frozen as ice. Scientists believe the last ice age ended ten to twenty thousand years ago.

As Earth's climate got warmer, much of the ice melted. The sea flooded low-lying coasts. Permanent flooding formed new regions of water and left areas of high ground sticking out as islands. The islands of Svalbard, Novaya Zemlya off Russia, and the islands of the Canadian Arctic **archipelago** formed in this way.

Arctic Coastlines

The long coastline of the Arctic Ocean stretches for more than 28,000 miles (45,000 km). The coastline of Russia is fairly jagged, cut by wide **estuaries**.

Fjords are a major feature that cut into the coasts of Norway, Greenland, and Alaska. These steep-sided inlets were gouged by **glaciers** during ice ages. As these huge rivers of ice neared the coast, they carved great, U-shaped valleys. Later, when the climate grew warmer, the glaciers melted and sea levels rose. The ocean flooded the valleys to form fjords.

The Arctic coast of Canada is edged by hundreds of islands, some of which are larger than the world's smaller nations. Even these big islands, however, are dwarfed by Greenland, the world's largest island, which covers 840,000 square miles (2,175,600 sq km).

Shaping Coastlines

Arctic shores have a wide range of coastal features, including sheer cliffs, rocky shores and headlands, sweeping bays, and wide **deltas**. The coastal landscapes of the Arctic are shaped by two main processes: erosion and deposition. Erosion is the wearing away of the land by water, wind, and other natural forces. Deposition is the laying down of rocky materials, often in the form of fine particles, such as sand, mud, or silt. Along Arctic coastlines, glaciers and ice sheets are important forces of erosion and deposition.

Waves are also a major force of erosion on coastlines. As they beat against the shore, they hurl sand and **shingle** against rocks to wear them away. Bands of hard rock at the water's edge are left to form jutting headlands, while soft rocks are eaten away to form curving bays. In some parts of the Arctic, waves are eating into coasts by 3 feet (1 m) or more each year, gradually shifting the shore inland.

Out to sea, the pounding waves smash rocky fragments into sand and shingle. Coastal **currents** may carry these materials for miles along the shore and then deposit them to form **barrier islands**, beaches, and **spits**. Elsewhere, at river mouths, **sediment** carried down by rivers is dropped to form flat, swampy deltas.

The flat, treeless lowlands of the tundra stretch down to the water's edge along many parts of the Arctic coastline. Beneath the top layer of soil, the ground is permanently frozen. In summer, when the snow and ice melt, water cannot drain away through the frozen subsoil, or **permafrost**. Instead, water pools at the surface, where it forms lakes and **marshes.**

Over a long period of time, waves have eroded these rocks on the Alaskan Peninsula into arches.

CHAPTER TWO

CLIMATE AND CURRENTS

Almost all of the Arctic Ocean lies within the Arctic Circle, which—at 66.5°N—forms the southern boundary of what is termed the polar region. The polar climate is harsh, with air temperatures reaching a maximum of 50° Fahrenheit (10° Celsius) in summer, and dropping to -40° F (-40° C) or below in winter.

Sun in the Arctic

The Sun has little warmth in the Arctic because it is never directly overhead. Because of the curvature of Earth, the Sun's rays have to travel a long way through the atmosphere to reach the ground in the Arctic. The rays are also spread over a wide area, which reduces their heating power.

Earth tilts on its axis as it moves around the Sun. In summer, the far north of the Arctic region is tilted toward the Sun and experiences periods of continuous daylight when the Sun never sets. For this reason, the Arctic is known as the "Land of the Midnight Sun." In winter, the far north is tilted away from the Sun and experiences continual darkness for long periods. The dark sky is sometimes brightened by the colorful lights of the aurora borealis.

Scarce Rainfall

Rainfall is scarce in the Arctic, with many parts receiving less than 10 inches (25 cm) of moisture yearly. Most rain or snow falls between spring and autumn; winter skies are usually clear. Rainfall is low in the Arctic, partly because the cold air can hold little moisture, but also because ice covering much of the ocean slows the process of **evaporation**. The floating ice reflects sunlight back into the air and prevents the water beneath the ice from evaporating.

The aurora borealis, also known as the northern lights, glow over the ocean off the coast of Alaska. These shimmering lights are caused by solar particles striking the atmosphere high above the Arctic Ocean.

Ice Shelves and Icebergs

There are two main forms of ice in the Arctic Ocean: sea ice (formed in the ocean), and land ice (formed from glaciers). Glaciers form on land in the Arctic when layers of snow get packed down and turn to ice. Greenland is mostly covered by an enormous, thick sheet of ice that slowly flows as glaciers from high ground in the center down toward the coasts. There, the ice forms huge, floating ice shelves extending out to sea, or it breaks off and crashes into the water to form icebergs.

There are two main types of icebergs. Tabular, or flat-topped, icebergs break

A glacier meets the ocean in the background of this photo. Land ice breaks off from the glacier to float as icebergs in the open ocean. Icebergs are not always white—they may be blue, green, or even black depending on their age, size, and the minerals in the ice.

The Water Cycle

Moisture continually circulates between the oceans, air, and land. This never-ending process, called the water cycle, is illustrated here. The Sun beating down on the ocean surface causes moisture to rise into the air in the form of a gas, water vapor. This process of turning liquid into gas is called evaporation. As the warm, moist air rises, it cools. Cold air can hold less mois-

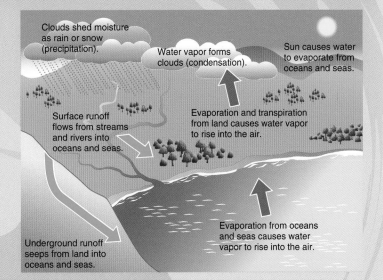

Clouds shed moisture as rain or snow (precipitation).

Water vapor forms clouds (condensation).

Sun causes water to evaporate from oceans and seas.

Surface runoff flows from streams and rivers into oceans and seas.

Evaporation and transpiration from land causes water vapor to rise into the air.

Underground runoff seeps from land into oceans and seas.

Evaporation from oceans and seas causes water vapor to rise into the air.

ture than warm air, and so the moisture in it **condenses** to form clouds, which may drift over the land before shedding rain. When rain falls on land, any moisture not absorbed by plants or soil drains away into streams and rivers. The water then runs into the ocean to begin the cycle again.

Plates of pancake ice (inset) form when waves push frazil ice together to form disks. These disks freeze together to form floes, such as those in the main photo. The fur seals visible here sit on floes when they want to get out of the water.

off from floating ice shelves. Smaller bergs, known as irregular icebergs, break off from glaciers at the coast and are weathered into a variety of shapes by wind and waves. Only about one-eighth of an iceberg's mass is above the ocean surface. The bulk lies below. Icebergs drifting south from the Arctic often menace ships, especially in the North Atlantic, before shrinking and, eventually, melting away in the warmer Atlantic waters.

Sea Ice

Most ice in the Arctic Ocean is sea ice, formed as the surface freezes over. Much of the Arctic Ocean has been covered by a thick layer of ice for thousands of years. In summer, ice continues to cover the northernmost areas of the ocean, those nearest to the North Pole, but the coasts of Alaska, Canada, Norway, and Russia become largely ice-free. In the fall, ice crystals begin to form at the surface in open water as the temperature drops, forming greasy-looking **frazil ice**. The ice gradually spreads southward to cover most of the Arctic Ocean in winter.

During winter, floating ice sheets called **floes** gradually thicken as more ice is added from below. Eventually, a thick crust called pack ice forms, up to 10 feet (3 m) thick in mid-ocean, and up to 6 feet (1.8 m) thick near coasts. Winds and currents may fold and pile the ice into tall, jagged ridges called pressure ridges. In some places, the same forces may break up the ice to create strips of open water named leads, or polynyas, up to 60 miles (96.5 km) across. When the weather warms in spring, the freezing processes of the winter are reversed, and the ice begins to thin again. Southern edges of the pack ice gradually melt and break up in the warmth of the sun.

Salt Levels

Salt content, or salinity, in the Arctic Ocean varies as the depth of water changes. When surface water freezes, the salt is driven out, and so the sea ice contains very little salt, especially if it is several years old. The salt that is driven out by the freezing process forms an extra-salty layer just below the ice, which then sinks because it is heavier than the surrounding water. Water in the ocean depths, therefore, is very salty. Where rivers flow into the Arctic Ocean, they

Why Is the Ocean Salty?

Ocean water is salty because it contains dissolved minerals, or salts, washed from the land by rivers or released underwater from hydrothermal vents and volcanic eruptions. The salt level in ocean water is higher than in rivers because, when surface water evaporates, the dissolved salts remain in the oceans and become more concentrated. Experts calculate that the salt in all the seas and oceans would be enough to bury Earth's landmasses to a depth of 500 feet (152 m)! So why do oceans and seas not get increasingly salty as new minerals are added each year? Some salt is removed from the water when it is absorbed by marine life or reacts with underwater rock and eventually forms new sediment layers on the ocean floor. These processes help keep salt levels constant in seas and oceans.

An iceberg protrudes from a large area of ice known as pack ice. Vast sheets of pack ice float across huge areas of the Arctic Ocean in winter.

This map shows the major surface currents of the Arctic Ocean and the main currents that flow into the ocean.

dilute coastal water with fresh water and make it less salty.

Feeding the Arctic

The landmasses enclosing the Arctic Ocean limit the exchange of water with other oceans. Sixty percent of the water entering the Arctic is Atlantic water brought in by the Norwegian Current. Pacific water, flowing through the narrow Bering Strait, contributes much of the remaining inflow. The ocean is also fed by large rivers, such as the Ob' and Lena in Russia and the Mackenzie in Canada.

Ocean Currents

Powerful winds blowing across the ocean drive surface currents and cause the water to flow in giant circles called **gyres**. In the Arctic Ocean, the huge, clockwise Beaufort Gyre circulates in the Canada Basin, while several smaller currents flow around coasts and islands.

Most of the cold water leaving the Arctic flows in a powerful current east of Greenland. This flow, which begins as the East Greenland Current, continues around the tip of Greenland and heads north, where it merges with water flowing south from Baffin Bay. These waters mix with currents from Hudson Bay to create the southward-flowing Labrador Current, which cools the eastern coast of Canada. Cold, dense water leaving the Arctic sinks as it meets the warmer, lighter waters of the Atlantic and Pacific, forming extremely cold bottom water in the two oceans. About 2 percent of water leaving the Arctic takes the form of icebergs drifting south in the Labrador Current.

Waves and Water Temperature

In areas of open water, strong polar winds may whip up towering waves. The ice that covers much of the ocean surface, however, prevents waves from breaking. Swells pass beneath the ice, rocking smaller floes and icebergs, but the water

beneath the ice is mostly calm, as well as dark and very cold.

Water temperatures vary little through the year, ranging between 28° F and 36° F (-2° C and +2° C) in different parts of the ocean. Although this is cold, water temperatures are nearly always warmer than air temperatures on the surround-

*Fishing vessels in Arctic waters have to contend not just with ice, but with strong waves in open areas that are free of ice. This **trawler** is in rough seas around Iceland.*

ing landmasses. The ocean, therefore, has a warming influence on the coasts that surround it, which is one reason why most Arctic settlements are on coasts.

What Causes Tides?

Tides are regular rises and falls in sea level caused mainly by the tug of the Moon's gravity. As the Moon orbits Earth, its gravity pulls ocean water into a mound below it. A similar bulge appears on the ocean on the opposite side of Earth because the planet itself is also being pulled, by the same force, away from the water on the far side. As Earth spins eastward, so the mounds move westward across Earth's surface, bringing tides to coasts in succession. Because Earth spins around once every twenty-four hours, the two bulges both move across Earth once in that period, creating two tides a day in each place.

The Sun's gravity exerts a similar, but weaker, pull on the oceans. This is because, while many times larger than the Moon, it is also much farther away. Every two weeks, at the full moon and again during the new moon, the Sun and Moon line up so that their pulls combine. This force brings extra-high tides called spring tides. They alternate with weaker tides also occurring every two weeks, named neap tides, when the two pulls tend to minimize each other. In the Arctic Ocean, the tidal range—the difference between high and low tide—is small to moderate, ranging from 1.5 to 16 feet (0.5 to 5 m).

CHAPTER THREE

MARINE LIFE

The Arctic is a harsh **environment**, and life there is most abundant in the warmer, shallow seas edging the ocean. Coastal **habitats** include extensive salt marshes—which attract nesting birds—and low, rocky shores where seals bask in summer.

Coastal Waters

Seaweeds waft in the shallows off some Arctic coasts of Europe and Greenland. Sea ice, however, can be a hazard in coastal waters. It grinds and scrapes along the bottom, making life impossible for seabed dwellers, such as starfish and sea urchins. In somewhat deeper waters farther out, colorful anemones, sea squirts, worms, clams, and sponges thrive on

the bottom, especially in places where currents bring nutrients. Many of these creatures are filter-feeders that sieve tiny plants and animals from the water.

Zones of the Open Ocean

Out in the open ocean, most life is found in the upper waters, or **euphotic zone**, which extends down 330–660 feet (100–200 m) from the surface. In open water, this oxygen-rich layer is bathed by sunlight in summer that supports floating plant **plankton** that provide food for shrimp and surface-dwelling fish. Plant plankton also grow on the bottom of thin sea ice but not under the thick ice in the center of the ocean. Whales, seals, and seabirds gather at leads, the strips of open water that provide them with good fishing areas.

Little light reaches the mid-depths, or **bathyal zone**, between 330–660 feet and 6,600 feet (100–200 m and 2,000 m) deep, particularly if ice covers the water. Without light, plants cannot thrive. Temperatures in this zone of

A view of the Arctic Ocean bottom shows mussels and sea urchins clinging to rocks.

the Arctic Ocean remain close to freezing throughout the year. Sperm whales and Greenland sharks are among the animals that visit this zone in search of fish, squid, and other prey. Sperm whales can dive to depths of 4,000 feet (1,200 m) and remain underwater for nearly two hours.

The jet-black waters of the **abyssal zone**, below 6,600 feet (2,000 m), are home to few animals. Deep-sea creatures survive here by feeding on the remains of dead plants and animals that sink down from above, or they prey on each other. Hydrothermal vents discovered on Mohns Ridge in 2005 are home to unusual species of shrimp, anemones, and sea spiders. Unlike almost all other living things, these deepwater creatures do not need oxygen or sunlight for survival, depending instead on bacteria.

Chain of Survival

Arctic habitats are extremely hostile in winter. For this reason, few creatures live here all year round. Many birds, mammals, and fish **migrate** to warmer seas in the fall to avoid the long winter months. In spring, they return to take advantage of the seasonal abundance of food, which is based on tiny plant plankton called diatoms. Starting in February, the lengthening

Some animals remain in the Arctic all year. Their white fur or feathers camouflage them against the ice. Shown here (from top to bottom) are: (1) a baby harp seal (which will become black and white when it matures), (2) a sleeping arctic fox, (3) a polar bear waiting for prey, and (4) ivory gulls perched on an iceberg.

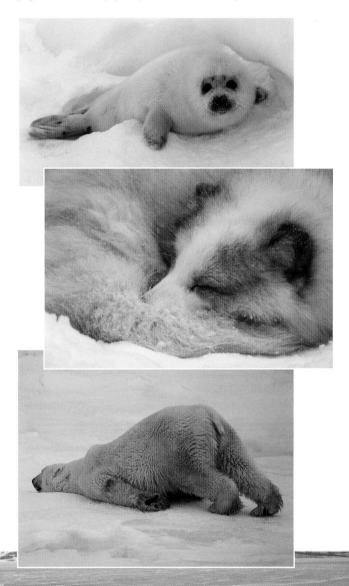

hours of daylight allow all plant plankton to **photosynthesize**, grow, and multiply, or "bloom." By March, diatoms form a brownish-yellow layer of **algae** up to 1 foot (30 cm) thick on the underside of the sea ice, and they also float in open water. Animal plankton, including small, shrimplike creatures called krill, feed on the algae. In turn, krill provide food for larger creatures in the Arctic Ocean, including the great whales.

A krill feeds on the algae growing under Arctic ice.

Ocean Food Chains

In the Arctic, as in other oceans, living things depend on one another for food. The relationships between plants and animals in a habitat can be shown in a food chain. Plants form the base of almost all marine food chains. Seaweeds and microscopic floating plants, or phytoplankton, use light to make their food, through the process of photosynthesis. Tiny animals called zooplankton, including krill and small fish, feed on plant plankton. They are eaten by larger creatures such as fish, seals, and whales. Orcas and polar bears are powerful hunters at the top of the Arctic food chain. When these and other living things die, their remains are eaten by shrimps, crabs, and microbes.

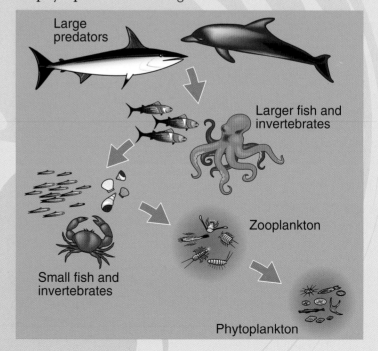

Large predators

Larger fish and invertebrates

Small fish and invertebrates

Zooplankton

Phytoplankton

A 1906 drawing from a U.S. Bureau of Fisheries bulletin shows a chinook salmon, an important fish for the Arctic commercial fishing industry.

Fish and Shellfish

Krill, shrimps, clams, worms, and starfish are all ectothermic, or cold-blooded. Ectothermic creatures have body temperatures similar to that of their surrounding environments. Many ectothermic species in the Arctic Ocean have adapted to the cold by living life at a slow pace. They move about very little and mature slowly, but they live for a long time—up to one hundred years in some species. During their long lives, some grow to giant size.

Fish are also cold-blooded, although they are active swimmers. The Arctic Ocean holds relatively few types of fish, with very few species inhabiting the central basin in the far north. Arctic cod pass the winter in northern parts of the Atlantic or Pacific Oceans. In spring, they swim into the central Arctic basin to feed on plankton at the edges of ice floes. Capelin, Arctic char, and salmon inhabit the warmer waters that border the ocean. Char and salmon swim up rivers to breed in streams on the tundra. Their young grow up and then swim out to sea.

Keeping Warm

Birds and mammals are endothermic, or warm-blooded animals. Endothermic animals maintain a warm, even body temperature whatever their surroundings. This process takes a lot of energy in cold places such as the Arctic, where the freezing air and water take body heat away fast. Arctic birds and mammals have to eat a lot of food, therefore, to provide energy for warmth. A dense coat of fur or feathers helps them stay warm. Seals, whales, and polar bears also have a layer of fatty blubber to provide extra insulation. Even so, most warm-blooded animals in the Arctic are migrants, visiting this cold region only in summer.

Birds of the Arctic

Ivory gulls and little auks are among the few birds that spend the whole year in the Arctic. Ivory gulls have a dense coat of white feathers. They live as scavengers, following predators, such as polar bears, to steal scraps from their kills. Little auks resemble penguins, but, unlike penguins, they are able to fly. They feed on plant plankton, which they store in small pouches on their throats.

For many types of birds, the Arctic, where food is plentiful in summer, provides a good place to rear their young. Guillemots, puffins, and terns arrive to breed in large, noisy groups on coasts. The Arctic tern is well known for its long-distance migrations. It breeds in the Arctic in spring and then flies all the way to the **Antarctic**, Earth's most southern region, to take advantage of the southern summer. Each year, these seabirds complete a round trip of up to 22,000 miles (35,000 km).

Many types of ducks, geese, and swans breed in the Arctic. Eider ducks nest on small islands where the females line their nests with soft down feathers plucked from their chests to keep their chicks warm. Brant geese arrive in June. Within two months, they nest, lay eggs, and rear their chicks before heading south again, this time migrating with their young.

Walruses

Walruses are members of the seal family. These enormous creatures weigh up to 3,000 pounds (1,360 kilograms). Half of this weight is the fatty blubber that keeps the marine mammals warm. The walruses' long tusks are a unique feature. Both males and females possess these extralong canine teeth, which can grow up to 35 inches (89 cm). Walruses use their giant tusks to stir up the seabed in search of shellfish and to haul their heavy bodies out onto the ice.

Walruses often huddle together for warmth and protection.

Arctic Mammals

Mammals of the Arctic Ocean include seals, whales, and polar bears. Many scientists class polar bears as marine mammals. These ferocious predators are equally at home on ice floes or in the water, where they swim with a strong paddle stroke. Polar bears feed mainly on seals. They spend hours lying in wait at holes in the ice where seals surface to breathe. When a seal pops up, the bear kills its prey with a single swipe of its massive paws.

Seals of Arctic waters include ringed seals, harbor seals, bearded seals, and walruses. Whales divide into two groups: toothed and baleen whales. Baleen whales are named for the bony fringes of baleen hanging down inside their mouths, which they use to sieve krill and small fish from the water. Baleen whales include blue and gray whales, which migrate to tropical seas

An orca whale, one of the many summer visitors to the Arctic Ocean, cruises an open lead in the pack ice, hunting for seals.

to breed in winter. Bowhead whales remain in cold waters throughout the year. They use their huge, domed heads to smash breathing holes in thick ice.

Toothed whales include the fearsome orcas that visit the Arctic in summer. Other toothed whales—belugas and narwhals—stay in cold seas all year round. Belugas live in large herds and are known as "sea canaries" because of the wide variety of sounds they make, including hoots, clangs, honks, and whistles. The male narwhal has a long, spiralling tusk growing out of its upper jaw. Experts believe these tusks are used to impress the females in the mating season. Long ago, narwhal tusks washed up on beaches may have given rise to the legend of the unicorn.

CHAPTER FOUR

PEOPLE AND SETTLEMENT

The Arctic Ocean has a warming effect on the lands around it, and so the climate on its coasts is milder than inland regions. For this reason, from earliest times, the peoples of the Arctic lived on coasts. The ocean also provided them with a rich source of food and a means of transportation. In winter, early Arctic peoples ventured far out on the sea ice while hunting. In summer, when the ice melted, they took to the water in boats.

Arctic Peoples

The Arctic coasts of North America and Greenland have been inhabited for thousands of years. The Native peoples of the Arctic—especially in North America and Greenland—used to be known as

Whale hunting was an important activity among the earliest settlers in and around the Arctic Ocean. This house on St. Lawrence Island, Alaska, was built with whale bones in a traditional Eskimo style.

During the last ice age, sea levels were much lower than they are today because so much water was locked up as ice. The Bering Strait, scientists believe, was not a stretch of water as it is now, but an area of land—known as Beringia—which formed a bridge between eastern Asia and North America. Many scientists believe that—about twelve thousand years ago or possibly even as early as thirty thousand years ago—modern humans started to move out of Asia across Beringia to reach North America. These migrations were probably triggered by the search for food, which had become scarcer because of cold temperatures. Later, as the climate warmed, sea levels rose and Beringia became the Bering Strait. Not all scientists agree on the dates and methods of the first human migrations—more recent theories say that people may have arrived in the Americas much earlier, and by other routes—but many are convinced that the Arctic region was among the first passages to those continents.

Eskimos. Today, the name Eskimo is still used in Alaska, but Native groups in Greenland and Canada are usually called Inuit. The Chukchi, Yakut, Samoyed, Nenets, and other groups were the first to inhabit the Arctic coasts of what is now Russia. The Aleut people lived in the Aleutian Islands and on the Alaska Peninsula. The Saami were the first people to live along Arctic coasts in Europe.

These peoples and other Native groups still live in the Arctic region. Many Arctic peoples keep alive the traditional ways of life of their ancestors.

The Inuit

In North America and Greenland, early Arctic peoples traditionally lived by hunting seals, whales, and other animals with **harpoons** and bows and arrows. They also speared fish and seals through holes in the ice. Seal meat was the most

important food. The Inuit word for seal, in fact, means "giver of life." The bones of marine animals made tools and weapons, their blubber was burned for heat, and their hides were used to make clothing.

Eskimo peoples traveled over the ice on sleds pulled by husky dogs. In summer, they hunted in coastal waters using canoes called kayaks. They lived in partially buried lodges made of stone and turf and roofed with whalebone rafters. They also built dome-shaped shelters, called igloos, using blocks of ice that they cut and stacked like large bricks.

The Saami and People of Russia

The Saami of northern Europe and the ancient peoples of Russia had a somewhat different lifestyle. They, too, lived by hunting and fishing, but they also herded reindeer, which provided meat,

A Nenets boy in Siberia prepares to lasso stray reindeer in his herd. The Nenets are traditionally a nomadic people, moving with the animals and the seasons.

milk, and hide. The deer also provided transportation as they were used to pull sleighs. In winter, the Nenets, Saami, and other groups moved south with the reindeer to shelter in inland forests. In spring, they moved their animals north to graze the pastures of the tundra, eventually arriving back at the Arctic coast.

Outsiders Come to the Arctic

During the 1600s, Europeans began to visit the Arctic region of North America, while both Russians and Europeans explored the wilds of Siberia. These people were the first outsiders to make contact with Arctic peoples. Newcomers were often amazed to find people living so far north and by their ways of life. One early visitor wrote of the Inuit: "Those

beasts, fishes, and birds which they kill are their meat, drink, clothing, bedding, shoes, and almost all their riches."

Trading and Trapping

In the late 1500s, European and Russian ships began to venture into icy Arctic waters in search of new sea routes that would lead to China and the East Indies, places that were important for trade. While these early attempts to find new shipping routes failed, the sailors returned home with tales of abundant whales, seals, and fur-bearing animals in the far north. Soon, hunters and traders from nations south of the Arctic were making regular trips to harvest these riches. Trading posts and whaling stations were set up on Arctic coasts.

In the 1700s, Russians crossed the Bering Strait to make contact and trade with the Native people of Alaska. They traded metal tools and weapons for the skins of foxes and sea otters trapped by Arctic peoples. By the early 1800s, a British business named the Hudson Bay Company had established a network of trading posts across northern Canada, and it controlled trade in the region. In 1867, the Russians gave up land claims and trading rights in Alaska when they sold the territory to the United States.

Changes for the Native Peoples

Trapping and trading soon became a way of life for Arctic peoples. As well as useful metal tools and cooking pots, the newcomers also brought liquor, tobacco, and new beverages and foods, such as tea and sugar. Arctic peoples grew to rely on these goods, and some became addicted to liquor. They were often treated badly by people who came from other areas. Some Native people were sold as slaves, while many died of new diseases, such as measles and tuberculosis, to which they had no resistance.

The discovery of gold in northern Canada and Alaska in 1896 had a huge impact on the Arctic region. Additional finds started a gold rush in 1897, with hopeful miners pouring into the region. Christian missionaries also arrived to convert local peoples to Christianity. These settlers had little respect for traditional Eskimo customs and beliefs.

Colonies and Settlement

By the early 1900s, all lands edging the Arctic Ocean had become **colonies**, claimed by bordering nations, including the United States, Canada, and Russia. Greenland had become a Danish colony in the 1700s. Arctic peoples had little say in the affairs of their own lands, and their minerals and other resources flowed south to other regions. Coal was mined on the islands of Svalbard and gold extracted from Nenets land in Siberia. Settlements grew up on Russian rivers emptying into the Arctic Ocean, and the ice-free harbors of Archangel

Whale stocks decreased dramatically with the invention, and introduction to the Arctic, of the harpoon gun. This photograph from a 1912 book about U.S. fisheries shows a harpoon gun used to kill whales.

With colonization of the Arctic, Murmansk—on the Barents Sea in Russia—became a center for trade. Today, it is a major port for the oil industry. The vessel shown here is used for storing oil in Murmansk harbor.

and Murmansk on the Barents Sea became bustling ports.

Military Bases

About the time of World War II (1939–1945), the Arctic Ocean took on a military importance to nations bordering the region. The United States, the Soviet Union, and Canada set up military bases and **radar** stations in the Arctic during the **Cold War**. Between 1945 and 1980, the number of bases there increased and provided work for local people. Some grew into towns.

Oil and Land Claims

In 1968, rich stocks of oil were discovered offshore at Prudhoe Bay in Alaska, and a mining town soon grew up there. Today, over six thousand oil industry workers are based at Prudhoe Bay at any one time.

From the 1970s, meanwhile, the Inuit and other groups began to demand a voice in how Arctic lands were run. They laid claim to areas where their ancestors had hunted for centuries. Several major land claims have since been settled in favor of Arctic peoples. In 1999, a vast territory in northern Canada called Nunavut was given over to Native groups, about 85 percent of them Inuit. This huge area covers 770,000 square miles (1,994,000 sq km) and includes Baffin and Ellesmere Islands.

Modern Settlements

The shores of the Arctic Ocean remain one of the most sparsely populated coastlines in the world. Nonetheless, tens of thousands of people now live and work on the Arctic coasts of Alaska, Canada, Greenland, Norway, and Russia. Some Arctic settlements are just small fishing villages. Others, such as Murmansk, are busy ports, while Prudhoe Bay in Alaska and Barentsberg on Svalbard are centers for mineral industries.

Constructing buildings on the frozen ground of the far north presents particular problems. Beneath the top layer of soil, the ground is permanently frozen as permafrost. The heat from houses and other buildings built on the permafrost can cause the frozen layer to melt, however, which makes buildings sink or tilt at crazy angles. For this reason, homes are sometimes built on metal frames that raise them off the ground, reducing heat flow to the frozen soil. The siting of telephone and electricity poles also presents problems. These poles are often set in concrete stands instead of into ground.

Igloolik

The small island of Igloolik lies off the shores of Foxe Basin in northern Canada. This region, north of Hudson Bay, is now part of the territory of Nunavut. Over twelve hundred people live in Igloolik's town, whose Inuit name means "many houses." The town has shops, a library, school, community hall, two churches, and good sports facilities. Homes, heated with electricity, are snug and warm. This small community, however, is still greatly affected by the climate. For ten months of the year, snow and ice cover the surrounding land and ocean, and Igloolik is largely cut off from the outside world.

This man is building an igloo using cut blocks of ice that he stacks and curves toward the center to form a domed roof.

CHAPTER FIVE

TRANSPORTATION AND COMMUNICATION

Kayaks

Inuit kayaks are light, maneuverable craft made of animal skins stretched over a bone or wooden framework. The slender boats, from 10 to 30 feet (3 to 9 m) long, are powered with a double-bladed paddle. Kayaks usually have watertight deck covers that fit around the sailor's body, protecting his or her bottom half as well as the boat's interior. The boats are light enough to be carried by one person over stretches of ice.

The Inuit kayak design was so successful that recreational kayaks are now seen on rivers and lakes worldwide.

The early inhabitants of the Arctic traveled over the ocean's ice in sleds hauled by huskies or reindeer. Today, sleds are more likely to be pulled by snowmobiles.

Inuit Boats

When coastal ice melted, early Arctic peoples skimmed the waters in one-person kayaks, hunting seals and small whales. The Inuit used bigger boats called *umiaks* when hunting large whales. These open boats carried up to ten people and were powered by oars and sometimes a sail. Craft of this size today are usually powered by outboard motors.

Vessels Made for Ice

From the 1500s onward, Europeans and Russians explored Arctic waters in multi-masted sailing ships. Many crews perished, however, when these wooden ships were trapped and crushed in the ice. From 1893 to 1896, a team of scientists, led by Norwegian explorer Fridtjof Nansen, carried out the first proper study of Arctic currents and drifting sea ice in a ship built to withstand the ice. Called the *Fram*, which means "forward," this vessel had sloping sides designed to ride up over the ice. It was partly powered by a windmill. On its three-year voyage, the *Fram* traveled right across the Arctic Ocean, carried by wind and ice. During the early 1900s, icebreakers began clearing the way for vessels carrying **freight** or passengers through the Arctic.

The Northeast and Northwest Passages

Not even icebreakers regularly smash their way across the central Arctic Ocean, which is covered by thick pack ice all year round. The only shipping routes lie in the outer parts of the ocean, close to the coasts of North America, Europe, and Asia. Starting in the 1500s, ships attempted to reach the Far East by traveling across the top of North America or Russia. The routes they tried were called the Northeast and Northwest Passages, and many ships were lost trying to find a way through these ice-choked waters.

The Northeast Passage was first completed by Swedish explorer Nils Nordenskjold in 1878–1879. The passage, now known as the Northern Sea Route, is in regular use thanks to a fleet of Russian icebreakers. Few ships travel all the way between the Atlantic and the Pacific Oceans, however. Most go part way to dock at ports on Siberian rivers, where they unload manufactured goods and take on timber, fish, and minerals.

An icebreaker has a specially reinforced, sloping bow that lifts the vessel up onto the ice as it moves forward. The weight of the icebreaker then breaks through the ice, clearing a path for itself and for other ships.

The Northwest Passage was eventually crossed by Norwegian explorer Roald Amundsen in a three-year voyage from 1903 to 1906. This route is too icebound, however, for ships to use regularly.

Submarine Travel

Submarines are the only vessels that can cross the central Arctic basin. They can do this because they travel beneath the ice, not through it. According to a U.S. Navy saying, "Only a fool would travel north of the Arctic Circle clad in anything less than a nuclear submarine." In 1958, the U.S. nuclear submarine *Nautilus* was the first vessel to travel under the North Pole. Less than one year later, another U.S. submarine, *Skate*, made the journey and actually surfaced at the North Pole through the ice.

During the Cold War period, U.S. and Soviet submarines prowled Arctic waters, playing cat and mouse with each other. When the Cold War ended, the U.S. Navy used its submarines to help civilian scientists carry out surveys of the Arctic Ocean. Named Scientific Ice Expeditions (SCICEX), the program lasted from 1995 to 2000 and led to many discoveries about the climate, ice, currents, water, and rock formations of the Arctic Ocean. Today, researchers use aircraft, **satellites**, land- and ice-based stations, and unmanned submersibles.

Eyes and Ears

"Going deep into the ocean using the eyes and ears of a Remotely Operated Vehicle always provides a new experience to me. Our recent dives in the Arctic also provide new information to scientists working to build our knowledge of these deep reaches. . . ."

Joe Caba, ROV pilot, Arctic Exploration expedition organized by NOAA in partnership with institutions in the United States, Russia, and China, expedition log, July 23, 2005

In 2005, an international expedition set out to explore habitats in the Arctic Ocean. They used a type of unmanned submersible, a Remotely Operated Vehicle (ROV), to take photographs and collect samples. ROVs are often used for research in dangerous ocean regions.

When the U.S. Navy submarine Honolulu *began surfacing near the North Pole in 2003, three polar bears came to investigate.*

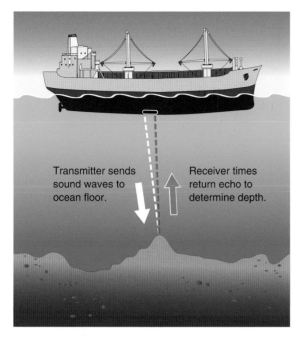

Sonar works with a transmitter that aims pulses of sound waves at the seabed. A receiver then times how long the echoes take to bounce back, and this indicates depth.

Navigation and Communications Systems

Modern vessels are equipped with a range of sensitive instruments that allow them accurately to locate their positions and **navigate** treacherous, icy waters. Sonar systems are used to measure depth and avoid dangerous reefs and shallows. Radar is used to detect sea ice, while small planes and helicopters often scout ahead to locate the open waters of leads. Ship-to-shore radio and satellite phones enable ships to receive weather forecasts. Modern compasses and global position-ing systems, using satellites, allow ships to pinpoint their positions.

Since the 1990s, the development of satellite telephones and radios—and the Internet—has revolutionized communica-tions in the Arctic. Even tiny settlements

on remote coasts and islands can remain in touch with the outside world when they are cut off by snow and ice.

Air Travel

Air travel offers a quick and relatively safe means of crossing the vast, icy wastes of the Arctic. The first airplane flight over the Arctic took place in 1926. Since the mid-1900s, planes and helicopters have been used to carry people and cargo to remote Arctic destinations. Planes flying commercial routes between western North America and Europe or Russia also regularly cross high above the ocean on routes running close to the North Pole. These aircraft pass well above the "bad weather zone" near ground level, where blizzards threaten planes taking off or landing at Arctic airports.

A traditional form of transportation is still effective in the remotest parts of the Arctic Ocean today—a team of husky dogs pulls a sled over rough ice during a polar expedition.

CHAPTER SIX

RESOURCES

The rich natural resources of the Arctic Ocean have been harvested for centuries. These harvests include fish and mammals as well as mineral wealth.

Whaling

Commercial whaling began in the Arctic as early as the 1500s. The industry was seasonal, taking place in summer when the southern ice melted. From small beginnings, the number of whaling boats in the region increased steadily. American whalers sailed there from North Atlantic ports, such as Nantucket and New Bedford.

Several parts of the whales were valuable—not just the meat, but the baleen from the great whales' mouths, which was used to make umbrellas, brushes, and ladies' corsets. Whale blubber was boiled down to make oil used for lighting lamps.

In the early days, whaling was highly dangerous. Sailors attacked whales from small, open boats with handheld harpoons, to which lines were attached, and then had to secure their lines if the giant creatures dived. By the late 1800s, the use of harpoon guns had made whaling easier. By this time, however, whales were very scarce in the Arctic Ocean. The whalers turned to other hunting grounds, such as the **Southern Ocean**. Eventually, whales became so scarce in all the oceans that commercial whaling was banned.

Sealing

Hunting seals was big business in the Arctic for hundreds of years. Sealskin was used to make warm coats, boots, hats,

Inuit people still use traditional Arctic resources. This man wears a seal fur coat to keep warm and hunts bowhead whales in a sealskin boat.

and gloves. The industry peaked in the 1960s and 1970s, when coats made of seal fur were fashionable. In the 1980s, however, conservation groups convinced many people that it was wrong to kill large numbers of seals for their fur, and seal coats went out of fashion. The sealing industry collapsed, and some species of seals have since begun to recover.

Commercial Fishing

The fishing grounds of the Arctic Ocean are less productive than other oceans.

Nonetheless, about 10 percent of the world's total fish catch is caught in the Arctic and in nearby seas, such as the Bering Sea. Cod and capelin are caught in the central Arctic basin or in the outer seas where they spawn. Halibut, plaice, herring, char, flounder, and shrimp are fished in outer Arctic waters, such as the Barents Sea, and in the neighboring Norwegian Sea. Salmon and char are caught or farmed in rivers.

Fishing fleets from Europe, North America, Russia, and Japan all operate

Traditional Whaling

The International Whaling Commission (IWC), which banned commercial whaling in the 1980s, allows certain Native groups in the Arctic to continue whale hunting on a very limited scale. This whaling is allowed for economic reasons— some small, remote communities are almost completely dependent on whaling for survival—and to preserve traditional ways of life. The IWC calls this hunting "aboriginal subsistence whaling."

A community on St. Lawrence Island, Alaska, starts to process a minke whale after a hunt.

From 1985 to 2002, about 5,650 whales were caught worldwide under the aboriginal subsistence allowance. In the Bering, Chukchi, and Beaufort Seas, for example, Alaskan Eskimos and the Native peoples of Chukotka in Russia are currently allowed to land a total of just sixty-seven bowhead whales in one year. Greenlanders, meanwhile, are allowed to catch nineteen West Greenland fin whales in any year. Some tribes and villages use modern equipment, such as motorized boats and bomb darts, in their hunts. Many, however, hunt by older methods, using umiaks and harpoons. Traditional ceremonies and festivals still accompany the catch in many regions.

of fish in a single haul. Stocks of Arctic cod and other species have dwindled because so many fish have been caught. Since the 1970s, fishing authorities, in an attempt to protect surviving stocks, have controlled the numbers of fish that can be caught.

Fishing Techniques

Commercial fleets and local fishermen use various techniques to net fish in Arctic waters. Trawl nets, shaped like giant funnels, are used to catch fish—including cod, haddock, and plaice—that dwell on the ocean bed. The wide mouth of the net is held open by **otter boards**, and trapped fish collect in the narrow, closed end of the funnel. Surface-dwelling fish, such as herring and mackerel, are caught in floating gill nets (flat nets that entangle fish) or purse-seine nets (nets that surround and enclose fish), while long lines are used to catch smaller numbers of cod.

in the Arctic. As in other oceans, Arctic fish are now threatened by **overfishing**. Before the invention of sonar, fishermen relied on their knowledge of weather, currents, and fish migrations to locate fish. Modern factory trawlers (trawlers that can freeze and store fish on board) are equipped with sonar to pinpoint fish, while their huge nets can land many tons

Mineral Resources

The discovery of gold in the Arctic region of North America and in Siberia brought hardship for some local peoples. Groups such as the Nenets were forced off their lands to make way for mines.

The Arctic Ocean itself holds rich reserves of other minerals, including coal, manganese, and tin. There is, at present, no practical way of mining these resources in the deep oceans, but drilling and **dredging** are possible in the shallows of the wide continental shelves. Gold, silver, lead, uranium, diamonds, and zinc are mined from the ocean or on Arctic coasts. Sand and gravel are also dredged for construction. Miners extract tin from the seabed off Siberia, while coal is mined on Svalbard.

Tourism

Tourism is a growing industry on the waters, coastlines, and islands of the Arctic Ocean. In summer, cruise ships bring tourists to photograph glaciers, whales, and seabirds, and a few hunters pay to go on polar bear hunts. All this provides work for local people, who act as wildlife guides and make clothes and carvings to sell as souvenirs.

Arctic Oil and Gas

Some of the world's greatest deposits of oil and natural gas lie on the floor of the Arctic Ocean. One of the world's largest natural gas fields is Shtokmanovskoye, of the coast off Russia in the Barents Sea. In 1968, after oil was discovered in Prudhoe Bay, Alaska, in the Beaufort Sea, a method had to be devised for exporting the oil. The seas around Prudhoe are icebound for much of the

The Trans-Alaska Pipeline snakes across the snow near Prudhoe Bay.

year, and moving the oil by **tanker** was not practical. In 1974–1977, the Trans-Alaska Pipeline was constructed to carry the oil right across Alaska to the North Pacific port of Valdez, which remains free of ice all year round. The bitter cold of winter, roaring winds, and shifting sea ice all make drilling for oil in the Arctic difficult and sometimes dangerous. Some oil rigs are sited on artificial islands made of gravel dredged from the seabed. Sometimes, drilling ships are used because they can be towed out of the path of the icebergs and ice islands that drift into coastal waters.

CHAPTER SEVEN

ENVIRONMENT AND THE FUTURE

The use of Arctic resources has led to some pollution in the region. Industries far to the south also pollute the polar environment of the Arctic.

Ocean Pollution

The low numbers of people living on the shores of the Arctic cause relatively little pollution. Industrial waste, however, pollutes mining areas and coastal waters around large ports, such as Archangel in Russia. On the islands of Svalbard, coal mining harms the habitats of seals and seabirds. In past times, unwanted chemicals, old oil rigs, and other junk were sometimes dumped in the ocean. Today, however, most nations bordering the Arctic Ocean have strict laws that control the dumping of waste.

Ocean currents waft waste chemicals from the Atlantic and Pacific Oceans into Arctic waters. For example, although there is almost no farming on the shores of the Arctic, **pesticides** reach Arctic waters from farms to the south. Once

An ice floe loaded with trash and waste from Barrow floats in the Arctic Ocean 80 miles (129 km) west of the city. This photo was taken in 1950; today, trash dumping is strictly controlled.

in the water, these chemicals are absorbed by plankton and krill and then passed on up the food chain to larger fish and shellfish. The chemicals build up in predators, such as seals, orcas, and polar bears, that eat poisoned prey.

The Threat of Oil Spills

In 1989, the export of Arctic oil through the port of Valdez, Alaska, led to a huge oil spill. When the oil tanker *Exxon Valdez* hit a reef in Prince William Sound, 11 million gallons (42 million liters) of crude oil spilled into the Pacific Ocean. Following the *Exxon Valdez* disaster, all new tankers have to be built with strong double **hulls**, which reduce the risk of oil spills. Old, single-hulled oil tankers are still in use, however. There have been no large oil spills from tankers in the Arctic Ocean, but as oil exploration and tanker traffic increases there, oil spills are considered one of the greatest future threats to the ocean.

Air Pollution

Chemicals from faraway industries can pollute the air in the Arctic. Waste gases, such as sulfur dioxide, drift north to form a dirty haze that hangs in the air. In 1986, the nuclear power plant at Chernobyl in Ukraine in eastern Europe caught fire and exploded. The explosion released a cloud of radioactive gas that

Coal mining at Uelen in coastal Siberia (shown here) causes water and land pollution in the region.

drifted all they way north to poison lichen and plants on the tundra in northern Europe and Russia. Thousands of reindeer that ate the vegetation were also poisoned and had to be destroyed.

High in the atmosphere, a layer of gas named the **ozone layer** protects people from the harmful ultraviolet rays in sunlight that can cause cancer and other health problems. In the 1980s, polar scientists discovered that the ozone layer above the Arctic and the Antarctic had thinned, allowing the harmful rays to get through. Experts quickly discovered that the ozone layer was being damaged by chemicals called chlorofluorocarbons (CFCs). These were used in refrigerators, spray cans, and foam packaging. Nations

Warming World

"The Arctic is experiencing some of the most rapid and severe climate change on Earth. The impacts of climate change on the region and the globe are projected to increase substantially. The Arctic is really warming now. These areas provide a bellweather of what's coming to planet Earth."

Robert Corell, Chairman of the International Arctic Science Committee that produced the Arctic Climate Impact Assessment report, November 2004

around the world eventually agreed to stop using the chemicals, and most make only CFC-free products, but the ozone layer will still take a long time to recover from the damage done by CFCs.

Conservation

Many Arctic creatures are now scarce because of overfishing, hunting, and pollution. Bowhead, blue, and fin whales have become very rare, but these huge mammals are now protected by the international ban on whaling. Walruses and polar bears were also threatened by hunting. Arctic Native peoples are allowed to kill a small number of whales, seals, and bears every year for their own needs. In general, however, hunting in the Arctic Ocean region is now tightly controlled.

Huge tracts of marine and coastal habitats in the Arctic have now been set aside as **nature reserves** and national parks. In these areas, mining and other activities that cause pollution are not allowed. One of the world's largest such reserves lies in northeast Greenland. Another huge reserve is the Arctic National Wildlife Refuge (ANWR), created when mining began in Prudhoe Bay in the 1960s. The refuge covers 20 million acres (8.1 million hectares) of coastal plain in Alaska and Canada. ANWR is home to **caribou**, polar bears, grizzly bears, musk oxen, and wolves. Parts of this wilderness, however, are now threatened by oil exploration. This activity could disrupt the habitats and migration routes of Arctic animals.

The Future of the Arctic Ocean

Because the world's climate is warming up, Arctic sea ice is melting at an astonishing rate, anything from 3 to 9 percent per decade, experts estimate. According to some scientific predictions, the waters of the Arctic could become ice-free for several months a year by the year 2100.

Far more than air pollution, waste, overfishing, and oil exploration, this climate change will affect the people, wildlife, and environment of the Arctic Ocean. If air temperatures in the region continue their gradual rise, the permafrost on which many Arctic buildings are constructed could melt, causing terrible problems for communities. When the permafrost melts, it may also release large amounts of methane, a **greenhouse gas**, into the air, creating further warming. As sea ice melts, Arctic animals, such as the polar bear, will lose their habitat. Shipping routes and even new fishing grounds will open up, increasing vessel traffic in the Arctic region. The melting of Arctic ice, however, does not just affect the ocean and the region around it. The changes it brings will have an impact on the climate of the whole world.

Global Warming

A climate change identified in recent years is affecting the world's oceans. World temperatures are slowly but steadily rising, in part because of air pollution from the burning of **fossil fuels**. Gases given off when these fuels burn trap the Sun's heat, producing warmer weather. The rising temperatures are warming the oceans, which makes the water expand and so raises sea levels. Sea ice is melting and now covers considerably less of the Arctic Ocean than it did forty years ago. Melting sea ice may affect the circulation of deepwater currents and affect the temperature of warm surface currents, such as the Gulf Stream in the Atlantic. These changes may have a dramatic effect on the climate of several nations. There are also signs that, as the Arctic and Antarctic regions warm, the land ice there—in the form of ice sheets and glaciers—is melting. This added water will cause sea levels around the world to rise dramatically, enough to swamp coastal areas. Many nations around the world, however, are making an effort to address global warming by reducing energy consumption and cutting down on air pollution.

The Arctic ice pack is getting smaller. This continuing change will have serious effects on Earth's climate.

TIME LINE

Before 20,000 years ago Saami people are living in Scandinavia; Chukchi, Nenets, Yakut, and other groups are living in Siberia.

About 20,000 years ago Eskimo peoples settle Arctic coasts of North America and Greenland.

Late 1500s–1600s Russians and Europeans begin to come to Arctic region.

1720s Russians and Europeans begin trading for furs with Native Arctic peoples. Denmark colonizes Greenland.

1867 Russia sells Alaska to the United States.

1878–1879 Nils Nordenskjold, Swedish explorer, is the first European to complete the Northeast Passage.

Late 1800s Invention of harpoon gun and boom in whaling industry lead to scarcity of whales.

1896 Discovery of gold in Canada and Alaska leads to gold rush.

1903–1906 Roald Amundsen, Norwegian explorer, is the first European to cross the Northwest Passage.

1926 First airplane crosses Arctic Ocean.

Early 1900s Sonar is developed.

1940s Scientists first chart Arctic Ocean floor using sonar and other devices.

1945–1980s United States, Canada, and Soviet Union build military bases across the Arctic.

1948 Scientists discover Lomonosov Ridge.

1958 U.S. submarine *Nautilus* travels under North Pole.

1959 U.S. submarine *Skate* surfaces through ice at North Pole.

1968 Oil is discovered at Prudhoe Bay on the Arctic Ocean, Alaska.

1974–1977 The eight hundred-mile Trans-Alaska Pipeline is constructed.

1977 Arctic Native peoples start reclaiming traditional homelands.

1980s Commercial whaling is banned worldwide by the International Whaling Commission.
Scientists discover thinning of ozone layer above Arctic and Antarctic.

1986 Accident at Chernobyl nuclear power plant in Ukraine in eastern Europe spreads radioactive pollution across part of Arctic region.

1989 Oil spill from *Exxon Valdez* pollutes coastline of Alaska.

1999 Territory of Nunavut is created in Canada for Native Arctic peoples.

2000 Scientists discover Arctic sea ice is thinning because of global warming.

2001 Scientists detect presence of hydrothermal vents along Gakkel Ridge.

2005 Hydrothermal vents and vent wildlife species are found on Mohns Ridge.

GLOSSARY

abyssal zone ocean below 6,600 feet (2,000 m)

algae tiny, simple plants or plant-like organisms that grow in water or damp places

Antarctic southernmost region of Earth that is the southern equivalent of the Arctic

archipelago group or chain of scattered islands

Arctic Circle imaginary line around the northern part of Earth at approximately 66.5°N

barrier island island lying parallel to the shore that protects mainland from the open ocean

bathyal zone mid-depths of ocean water between 330–660 feet deep and 6,600 feet deep (100–200 m deep and 2,000 m deep)

caribou large deer found in the Arctic regions of North America (known as reindeer in European and Asian Arctic)

Cold War period of rivalry between 1945 and 1991 among communist nations and western capitalist nations, fueled mainly by hostility between the United States and Soviet Union

colony territory claimed by a nation or area occupied by settlers

condense change from gas into liquid

continental drift theory that landmasses are not fixed but slowly drift across Earth's surface because of tectonic plate movement

current regular flow of water in a certain direction

delta land composed of mud and sand deposited around the mouth of a river

dredge gather by scooping up or digging out

environment surrounding conditions in which living things exist

estuary area of water at a coastline where a river meets the ocean

euphotic zone upper layer of ocean water, usually defined as above 330–660 feet (100–200 m)

evaporation process of change from liquid into gas

fjord deep, steep-sided inlet gouged by a coastal glacier and later flooded by water

floe floating sheet of ice

fossil remains of plants or animals preserved in rock

fossil fuel coal, oil, natural gas, and other fuels formed in the ground from remains of plants or animals

frazil ice small ice crystals on the surface of water that freeze together to form a layer of slushy ice that is the first stage of sea ice

freight cargo transported by sea, air, rail, or road

glacier mass of slowly moving ice on land

greenhouse gas gas, such as methane or carbon dioxide, that traps heat in Earth's atmosphere, contributing to global warming

gyre surface current in an ocean or sea that moves in a clockwise or counterclockwise circle

habitat type of place, such as a mountain or coral reef, where plants and animals live

harpoon type of spear used for hunting large fish and whales

hull body of a ship. Some vessels have two hulls, joined by a deck or other structure, for stability.

hydrothermal vent hot spring found in volcanically active parts of the ocean floor

lava hot, melted rock on Earth's surface that has welled up from under the ground

magma molten rock beneath the surface of Earth

mantle part of Earth between the crust and core. It is mostly solid rock, but part of it is molten.

marsh wet, usually grassy land

migrate move from one place to another

mineral natural, non-living substance

nature reserve place kept as wilderness habitat for animals and plants

navigate use animal instinct or scientific skills to determine a route or steer a course on a journey

otter board flat piece of wood or metal used to hold open a trawl net

overfishing catching so many fish that stocks are depleted or species made extinct

ozone layer layer of Earth's upper atmosphere with high levels of ozone, a form of oxygen

peninsula piece of land jutting out into water but connected to mainland

permafrost permanently frozen ground found beneath top layer of soil in very cold regions

pesticide chemical used to kill insects and other pests that harm crops

photosynthesize use carbon dioxide, hydrogen, and light to produce food, as plants do

plankton microscopic plants (phytoplankton) and animals (zooplankton) that float at the surface of oceans and lakes and provide food for many larger animals

radar system that detects and locates objects by bouncing radio waves off them

ridge raised area on land or on ocean bottom

rift opening on land or in the ocean where the ground has split apart

satellite vehicle that orbits Earth that can be used to send signals to Earth for communications systems; or any object in space that orbits another, larger object

sediment loose particles of rocky material, such as sand or mud

shingle deposit of small rocks, like large gravel, usually found on coastlines

sonar (short for sound navigation and ranging) system that uses sound waves to measure ocean depth and detect and locate underwater objects

Southern Ocean body of water, larger than the Arctic Ocean, that surrounds the continent of Antarctica in the far south of the world

spit long, narrow finger of land stretching out into water

strait water channel that connects two areas of water

subduction zone region where two tectonic plates press together, causing one to subduct, or dive below the other

submersible small underwater craft often used to explore deep parts of the ocean

tanker ship fitted with tanks for carrying liquid

trawler fishing vessel that drags a large net to catch fish

tundra land in cold regions, such as the Arctic, with no trees and permanently frozen subsoil (permafrost)

FURTHER RESOURCES

Books

Cole, Melissa. *Arctic*. Wild America Habitats (series). Blackbirch Press, 2003.

Haslam, Andrew. *Arctic Peoples: The Hands-On Approach to History*. Sagebrush, 2002.

Hoyt, Erich. *Whale Rescue: Changing the Future for Endangered Wildlife*. Firefly Animal Rescue (series). Firefly Books, 2005.

Litwin, Laura Baskes. *Matthew Henson: Co-Discoverer of the North Pole*. African-American Biographies (series). Enslow Publishers, 2001.

Santella, Andrew. *The Inuit*. True Books: American Indians (series). Children's Press, 2000.

Somervill, Barbara A. *Animal Survivors of the Arctic*. Watts Library (series). Franklin Watts, 2004.

Tocci, Salvatore. *Arctic Tundra: Life at the North Pole*. Franklin Watts, 2005.

Warrick, Karen Clemens. *The Perilous Search for the Fabled Northwest Passage*. In American History (series). Enslow Publishers, 2004.

Web Sites

The Arctic Ocean
www.aquatic.uoguelph.ca/oceans/oceanframes.htm

Defenders of Wildlife—Marine
www.defenders.org/wildlife/new/marine.html

How NASA Studies Water
kids.earth.nasa.gov/water.htm

Volcanoes, Earthquakes, Hurricanes, Tornadoes
www.nationalgeographic.com/forcesofnature/interactive

What's the Story on Oil Spills?
response.restoration.noaa.gov/kids/spills.html

WWF Habitats Home
www.panda.org/news_facts/education/middle_school/habitats/index.cfm

About the Author

Jen Green worked in publishing for fifteen years. She is now a full-time author and has written more than 150 books for children about natural history, geography, the environment, history, and other topics.

INDEX

ML

5/06